THIS BOOK
BELONGS TO

Becca

Henriette Ronner.

CATS

IN WORDS AND PICTURES

FOUR SEASONS
PUBLISHING LIMITED

CATS

How many times have I rested
tired eyes on her graceful little body,
curled up in a ball and wrapped
round with her tail like a parcel;
or stretched out luxuriously on my bed,
one paw coyly covering her face,
the other curved gently inwards
as though clasping an invisible treasure.

AGNES REPPLIER

❉

CATS

CLEAN AS A NEW PIN
George Hillyard Swinstead
1860–1926

CATS

TAKING A CAT NAP
Henriette Ronner-Knip 1821–1909

When I play
with my cat, who knows
whether I do not make
her more sport than she
makes me?

MICHEL DE MONTAIGNE

It has been the
providence of Nature to
give this creature nine
lives, instead of one.

A tough
neighbourhood is one
in which any cat
with a tail is a tourist.

❊

CATS

STILL LIFE WITH CAT AND MOUSE
Anonymous

❊

CATS

The cat that always wears silk mittens
Will catch no mice to feed her kittens.

ARTHUR GUITERMAN

There is, indeed,
no single quality of the cat that man
could not emulate to his advantage.

CARL VAN VECHTEN

Cats seem to go on the
principle that it never does any harm
to ask for what you want.

JOSEPH WOOD KRUTCH

❖

CATS

Even in Europe
the cat's cry is 'meow'.

CEYLONESE PROVERB

Cats know how
to obtain – food without
labour, shelter without
confinement, and love
without penalties.

WALTER LIONEL GEORGE

You can't look at a
sleeping cat and feel tense.

JANE PAULEY

THE FAVOURITE
Wilhelm Schutze 1840–1898

CATS

BATH TIME
Adrienne Lester 19th century

CATS

Cruel but composed and bland,
Dumb, inscrutable and grand,
So Tiberius might have sat
Had Tiberius been a cat.

MATTHEW ARNOLD

A cat can be trusted
to purr when she is pleased,
which is more than can be said
for human beings.

WILLIAM RALPH INGE

❋

All thoughts of mouse safaris
And tiger hunts have fled,
Pampered puss is home again
Asleep upon the bed.

W. GIRT

※

THE FISHING PARTY
Horatio Henry Couldery b.1832

I can rarely remember
having passed a cat in the
street without stopping to
speak to it.

BRUCE MARSHALL

CATS

Nature's links are being broken.
Love your feline jungle token.
Ring out the purrs, MagnifiCAT!
There's no such thing as a common cat.

BARBARA JOYCE

God made the cat
in order that man might have
the pleasure of caressing the tiger.

FERNAND MERY

No favour
can win gratitude from a cat.

JEAN DE LA FONTAINE

❊

THE ARTIST'S ASSISTANT
Marie Sophie Goerlich fl. 1880–1890

✳

CATS

CAT PLAYING BANJO ON BEACH
SURROUNDED BY ADMIRING KITTENS
Ernest Nister c.1898

CATS

Cat: a pygmy lion,
who loves mice, hates dogs,
and patronizes human beings.

OLIVER HERFORD

A kitten is the delight of a household.
All day long a comedy is played out
by an incomparable actor.

CHAMPFLEURY

A cat sleeps fat,
yet walks thin.

FRED SCHWAB

MOTHER'S LOVE
Henriette Ronner-Knip 1821–1909

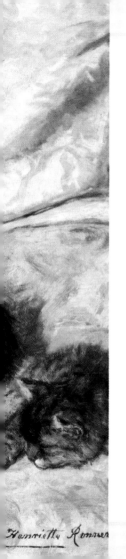

CATS

A dog is a dog,
a bird is a bird,
and a cat is a person.

MUGSY PEABODY

A kitten is the most irresistible
comedian in the world.
Its wide-open eyes gleam
with wonder and mirth.

AGNES REPPLIER

A sleeping cat is ever alert.

FRED SCHWAB

Cats are a mysterious
kind of folk.
There is more passing in their
minds than we are aware of.

SIR WALTER SCOTT

CATS

For me, one of the pleasures
of cats' company is their
devotion to bodily comfort.

COMPTON MACKENZIE

His friendship is not easily won
but it is something worth having.

MICHAEL JOSEPH

If a cat does something,
we call it instinct;
If we do something
for the same reason,
we call it intelligence.

WILL CUPPY

❊

CATS

PUSS IN BOOTS

If man could be crossed with the cat,
it would improve man but deteriorate the cat.

MARK TWAIN

❄

CATS

A HAPPY FAMILY
Eugene de Blaas 1843–1931

❊

CATS

I love cats because I enjoy my home;
and little by little, they become its visible soul.

JEAN COCTEAU

In a cat's eyes,
all things belong to cats.

PROVERB

Nothing's more playful than a young cat,
nor more grave than an old cat.

THOMAS FULLER

People meeting for the first time
suddenly relax if they find they both have cats.
And plunge into anecdote.

CHARLOTTE GRAY

❄

CATS

Purring would seem to be, in her case,
an automatic safety-valve device
for dealing with happiness overflow.

MONICA EDWARDS

The cat may look at a king they say,
But rather would look at a mouse at play.

ARTHUR GUITERMAN

There are no ordinary cats.

COLETTE

There is nothing
in the animal world, to my mind,
more delightful than grown cats at play.
They are so swift and light and graceful,
so subtle and designing, and yet so richly comic.

MONICA EDWARDS

A SWEET TORTOISESHELL
Charles van den Eycken 1859–1923

ALSO IN THIS SERIES

Dogs — In Words and Pictures
Golf — In Words and Pictures
Women — In Words and Pictures

Published by

FOUR SEASONS
PUBLISHING LIMITED

LONDON, ENGLAND

Text research by *Pauline Barrett*
Designed in association with *The Bridgewater Book Company*
Edited by *David Notley* and *Peter Bridgewater*
Picture research by *Vanessa Fletcher*
Printed in Dubai

ISBN 1-85645-506-8

ACKNOWLEDGEMENTS

Four Seasons Publishing Ltd would like to thank all those
who kindly gave permission to reproduce the words and visual
material in this book; copyright holders have been identified
where possible and we apologise for any inadvertent omissions.

We would particularly like to thank the following
for the use of pictures: *Bridgeman Art Library, e.t. archive,
Fine Art Photographic Library.*

Front Cover and Title Page: KITTENS, *Fannie Moody* fl.1885–1897
Endpaper: STUDIES OF CATS, *Henriette Ronner-Knip* 1821–1909
Frontispiece: A PAMPERED PET, *Henriette Ronner-Knip* 1821–1909
Back Cover: BATH TIME, *Adrienne Lester* 19th century

Henriette Ronner.

95.